VOYAGES

Stephen Brooke

Eggshell Boats
2017

Voyages
©2017 Stephen Brooke

Some men may seek the distant shore

All rights reserved. The text, art and design of this publication are the copyrighted work of Stephen Brooke and may not be reproduced nor transmitted in any form without the express written permission of the author or publisher, other than short quotes for review purposes.

ISBN 978-1-937745-46-2

Eggshell Boats
is an imprint of the Arachis Press

Arachis Press
4803 Peanut Road
Graceville, FL 32440
http://arachispress.com

VOYAGES

SHIP

It is my ship, this poetry,
the ship I sail upon a sea
of words. I seek your unknown lands,
uncharted golden virgin sands
that swim along the edge of dream.
How often has some distant gleam
ensorcelled me? Mirage and mist—
the hidden realms of alchemist
or wizard lie a league beyond
horizons where tomorrow dawned.
Ah, yes, such vision fades and fails
yet new winds rise to fill the sails
of this, my ship, my poetry,
to voyage in discovery.

TO SEA ONCE MORE
a song

The sea's awakened in my heart,
I can not stay ashore.
My love, it's time that we must part;
I'll go to sea once more.
A wind in my soul has broken free,
And bears me from my home;
Await me by the cold gray sea
As long as I must roam.

Can your love carry me across the sea,
Back to the land that gave birth to me?
Cry no more, what must be will be:
A sailor's heart must sometimes be set free.

Long bridled winds are rising free
To bear me from my home;
Await me here beside the sea
As long as I must roam.
My ship sails on the morning tide,
Bound for some distant shore;
But I'll return and here abide
And go to sea no more.

VOYAGES

Where pass the ones we loved?
Their memory must slip
across our each horizon,
become a foreign land

where we may voyage no more.
And should we glimpse some sail
across a misted gulf,
ask not what harbor

it seeks, what lands of gold
and innocence lie there.
They are not for us;
no, not any longer.

JEREZ

Her voice has the color of wine,
so I must a drunkard be,
quaffing deep of desire,
born beyond the sea.
And when my goblet's emptied,
down to the bitter lees,
I'll ask for more of that vintage—
another bottle, please!

DEPTHS

What seas I've sailed seem merely ponds
beside the ocean that is you,
and I, a lad, have sailed toy boats
with dreams of undiscovered blue

depths, found now within your eyes.
Might I win treasure there beyond
these coasts I've charted, oh, so well?
For I am but a vagabond

sailor on the seas of life;
should I dare plunge into you?

TIDES

The tides of the heart
follow no phases
of the moon, no
calendar of spring
and neap. They run high
when they will.
They leave the pools
of yesterday
to greet the sky,
the sky of stars
and starfish. Seek
with me there,
some night, for both.

FULLNESS

As the sail embraces the wind,
I shall take the fullness of you;
take it into myself and be
driven across what seas you will.

As the night must dream of dawn,
I'll seek visions in your arms
and count each star that climbs the dark
as prophecy of you, my morn.

As the pool has known the sky
in its mirrors of a moment,
I'll reflect both light and shadow;
I'll accept all that is you.

EACH

Each storm that passes, wind that blows,
repeats the message my heart knows;
each sullen beat that fills my veins,
the blood that burnt for you remains.

Each curtain closed, each door I latch,
each distant song I strain to catch,
each setting sun, each moon that wanes,
the memory of you remains.

Each falling star, each fading dream,
each useless wish, unlikely scheme,
each empty night, each day that rains,
the love I had for you remains.

SOUTHERN SEAS
a song

Long ago, in a northern land,
the outbound tide called me
to come and watch the hot red sun
rise o'er a tropical sea.

And though no more than a country lad,
sixteen and alone,
I found my way down to a port,
gray with fog and stone.

A tall ship beat up from the south,
sails spread like white doves' wings,
with cargo of spice and bales of silk,
the treasure of savage kings.

So I shipped aboard and we sailed away
to the southern seas and beyond;
we sailed out of an amethyst eve
and into a golden dawn.

Like some ancient god's forgotten gems,
islands I have seen
scattered shining in the surf,
emerald on aquamarine.

Now I've not looked back nor have I voyaged
again to my cold birth land;
I made the southern seas my home,
with their corals and silvered sands.

Till I came to anchor in a lost lagoon
and watched the seabirds soar;
then traveled no more but lived out my life
upon its jungled shore.

THE MERMAN'S LOVE

From what dark and unknown depths did you arise,
My lost merman paramour with sea-hued eyes?
Do you gambol now through kelpy arches there,
Playing hide-and-seek with lissom mermaids fair?
Think, sometime, of she who pines for you above
And, once more, swim up to me, your mortal love.
I await your coming by the sunset sea,
Walking empty shores till you return to me.

THE OTHER WOMAN

The ocean is the other woman in my life.
She calls me from your side, yes, whispers her way through
my dreams upon a breeze, salt-scented, from the south.
And though dreams they may be I must believe them true.

Let me leave behind this fog of Northern ports.
Let me seek the sun once more and do not be
jealous of my love, for she will cast me back
upon your shores, some day, the fickle, faithless sea.

Yes, a faithless lover the ocean ever is
and man was never meant to seek her as a wife.
He'll yearn and find no peace, sailing ever on;
yet she remains the other woman in my life.

DEEPER

Such tides,
such tides,
carry me

on the breath
of the moon.

I drown
in this sky
deeper than oceans.

TERRA INCOGNITA
a song

Voyage ended, I study maps
and ponder unknown lands.
They call to me, my restless heart
remembers trackless sands.
Across the leagues, a whispered song
trembles on the air;
it holds the voice of the lonely gull,
o'er seas where no men fare.

I've known the sun of tropic morns,
that rips the horizon asunder,
and lightning fierce as tigers' claws,
the roaring of its thunder.
Dropped anchor in the sapphire depths,
off teeming sun-gold ports,
or jungled shores where gem-clad kings
hold sway in savage courts.

In search of Terra Incognita,
I will sail afar
to lands beyond the lands I know,
beneath an unnamed star.
There is a life yet undiscovered,
a world to explore—
I search for Terra Incognita,
I search for my lost shore.

The wooden ribs of this cold room
are now my ship, it seems,
and in place of snowy sails,
I have but my dreams.
Chair and chart, I long to plot
an ending to my tale;
there comes the day I take the helm
and into dawn I sail.

PORTS

Morning was full of sun, as hot and golden
as Madras curry, the sky as deep as oceans,
and the ocean as deep as eternity.

The wind wrote messages across the sails,
wrote with the wings of seabirds, dipped in salt,
of harbor just beyond my world's edge.

Every port will have its name, its face,
as familiar as yesterday, as full
of promise as the dawn—the wharves, the taverns,

the women of the darkened, winding ways.
Ah, the women —their names and faces fade,
fade like the ebb tide on those distant shores

called home. Will I find the arms of either
at voyage's end? They are the dreams of star-filled
watches and songs half-heard upon the night.

And night is deeper than oceans, deeper yet,
and blacker than the pepper of Malabar,
spread before the buyers in the market.

AND THE SEA

Of life and death and the sea I shall speak,
of those who wander and those who seek
the further shores of eternity,
coasts of what is and of what can be.

Of fickle winds, the phantom shore
we once might glimpse and see no more,
I'll speak of these, though I know naught
beyond the dreams where I have sought

the golden sands no man has trod,
a paradise known only to God,
yet one thing I can tell you, Mate,
we're all adrift on the Seas of Fate.

Aye, many a searcher gallantly sailed
and every man of them has failed,
yet sailed on knowing full the cost
of seeking still for that they lost

on voyages past. Beneath a vault
of troubled sky, the scent of salt
upon the wind, I knew the sun
of other lands, of days undone.

I speak of life and death and the sea,
what never was, what never can be—
there's one thing I can tell you, Mate,
we're all adrift on the Seas of Fate.

THE WIND ON THE PRAIRIE, THE WIND ON THE SEA
a song

The wind on the prairie, the wind on the sea,
the wind swept away all that's left of me,
away across the ocean wide,
away across the great divide.
The wind will never let me be—
the wind on the prairie, the wind on the sea.

The wind of morning called one day,
whispering of a distant shore,
and the wind carried me away,
away from a home I'll see no more.
Oh, that wind, it knew my name
and it promised to make me whole;
Yes, it called me and I came,
called out to my restless soul.

Across the restless waters it blew,
wrote a fortune in sea foam;
my heart told me it was true—
with the wind I'd ever roam.
Weary, I have sought to rest,
sheltered in some headland's lee;
the crying gull above the wave's crest
calls me to my destiny.

Once I was a cowboy, riding,
Silver spurs hung at my heels;
painted stallion beneath me striding,
going to find what dawn reveals.
Yes, I rode a fine tall horse
across a wide and empty land,
followed a river to its source,
where the snow-gripped mountains stand.

Wagons rolled across the plains,
storms rolled above the broad expanse,
and I faced the droughts and rains,
watched a distant devil dance.
Their canvas gleamed like snowy sails
on a sea of grass, wind-swept,
and all of my forgotten tales
night sang to me as I slept.

Every ship needs sails and anchor,
every bird both earth and sky,
and this heart at times must hanker
to see my home before I die.
What compass points to all I've lost,
on what tides should I now sail?
What divides must yet be crossed,
how long must the winds yet wail?

Far across the mountain heights,
prairies where the lost winds weep,
across the vast and starry nights
I've watched rise from the oceans deep,
could I find familiar sands,
where I once dreamed on the shore,
might I find the distant lands
where I hear the wind no more?

The wind on the prairie, the wind on the sea,
the wind swept away all that's left of me,
away across the ocean wide,
away across the great divide.
I pray for that wind to set me free—
the wind on the prairie, the wind on the sea.

BOUND

To watch the stars one must first find
firm footing, lest they spin, unfixed,
in heaven, all their purpose lost.

For understanding has its cost
and even freedom is defined
in closed and well-bound dictionaries.

Yet I have been the fool who tarries
to sort the gifts, when they seem mixed;
unsure, unguided, misaligned,

I've sought the stars as one who's blind.

NAME

I will give your name to a Bedouin tribe
so they may carry it into the desert,
write it on the sands for God to read.

An unbelieving wind sweeps clean my world.
I have felt its lies; I've whispered them
to the evening star, and watched her fade.

I will set your name upon some ship
that sails westward into faceless night;
there I'll find you, written upon the waters.

PRODIGAL

I have squandered my estate
for a moment's pleasure,
the flickering lifetime
of posture and lie.

The prodigal must return
or his tale is unfinished.
Will I be seen on the road
and thought but another beggar?

Only when I no longer
desire this earth
shall I come into my inheritance,
that kingdom promised

the meek and the poor.

GRAINS OF SAND

I have been in the desert,
counting the grains of sand.
They mark the days of exile.
They whisper in the night
of an oasis.

She is there, say the dunes,
shifting ever slowly.
*Among the palms shall you
find her, and she will feed you
of the sweet dates.*

As a wandering tribe
I passed from land to land.
Where does tomorrow grow,
I asked, *beside shaded waters?*
None could say.

Further on, they tell me.
They point to the setting sun.
*There lie all the wonders
we fear to seek, as many
as grains of sand.*

All I had has blown
away, crossed that horizon.
The desert has no end.
I have counted the grains
of sand, and know.

SUITCASE

I've read that if an actor
who carries a suitcase on stage
is to give an honest performance
he should know exactly what
he has packed, where he is bound,
even if it's empty and he's only
crossing the stage.

I am that actor, crossing
my stage, my empty suitcase
filled with poems. Allow me
to open it and pull out one more
as I continue toward my destination.

BAG

The way to Paradise is littered
with discarded sins, the luggage
we once thought we needed.

Drop that bag by the roadside;
you need carry it no further.
It's become no more

than a burden and, you know,
we need not pack so much
for our journey home.

WARE
a sonnet

The truth of every day is bought and sold
in bright bazaars that entertain the crowd,
with barkers' urgent voices rising loud
lest by some chance a different tale be told.
Hear us! they cry, for all you need we hold—
this and no more than this may be allowed,
and any other swiftly disavowed
as we our lurid tapestries unfold.

Go find forgotten corners of the square
and gather up the words that lie there lost;
I'll fashion songs of them and night's dark air,
hold each, remembering what it once cost.
What coin for those with such fine unsold ware?
Only the shining pennies children tossed.

CLIMB

God may not wait
atop this mountain
but the devil's surely
back there behind me.

Keep climbing. Keep climbing.
The air grows cold
and more clear;
the summit is not far.

Life and death have held
the ends of my rope.
Keep climbing. The wind
will sweep all clean.

SING NO MORE

I will sing no more on the mountain;
I will sing no more of you.

The rocks have held me, dreaming,
as I wept in their arms.
The high snows are streaming
to a distant sea.

I will sing no more with my friends;
I will sing no more of you.

My heart has sailed away
on last night's full moon,
all that was yesterday
afloat upon its tides.

I will sing no more of tomorrow;
I will sing no more of you.

Sea and sky have faded
each into the other.
The dawn would bring you to me;
you wore the scent of gardens.

I will sing no more in the valleys;
I will sing no more of you.

Once night threw stars at me
as I slept in your arms.
You and I have faded
each into the other.

I will sing no more love.
I will sing no more of you.

RIVERS
a sijo

We flow through deserts of time, you and I,
rivers destined for an unseen sea.

These banks are too high for any flood,
rage though we might between them.

One day, you will know me as the rain,
remembering its way home.

BUTTERFLY HEART

My butterfly heart
is not for your net;
it will flutter free
a day or two yet.
Though many a maid
has eagerly sought
my butterfly heart,
it's never been caught.

My butterfly heart
must be with the breeze,
for zephyrs of spring
to waft where they please,
and dance on bright wings
from sunrise to set;
my butterfly heart
is not for your net.

STOPS

There are no destinations,
only stops along
the way to nowhere.

Rest here with me a while
before we journey on.

CROSSED
a sijo

Our highways crossed as we
traveled toward the dawn.

Did you glance into your mirror
and see me as I paused?

These what-ifs and might-have-beens
overflow my box of dreams.

THE ROAD

Some say the journey
matters and not
the destination.

They never traveled
the road to you.

Each mile, each day,
brings me closer
to my heart's rest.

BARGAINS
a song

There are no love songs in my heart,
none left to beguile;
I sold them all to pretty girls
for a kiss and a smile.
And at the time, each bargain made
seemed more than worthwhile,
But now I've not one love song left,
not one song to beguile.

And each and every pretty girl,
each girl I have known,
Took away one verse of my heart
and kept it as her own.
Oh, there's no doubt I loved them all,
though memory has flown;
So who's to say who got the bargain,
I or the girls I've known.

There are no sorrows in my heart,
I'll not regret one song,
Sold to please a smiling face—
in that I find no wrong.
Or win the heart of a pretty girl,
for that's where they belong,
But now I have no more songs left,
no, not one love song.

OCCASIONAL FORTUNE
a song

I might be quite disappointed,
were I not a pessimist born,
by how things will often turn out—
I'd hang my poor head and I'd mourn.
But, ever expecting the worst,
I'll readily raise a glass
in toast to occasional fortune,
good luck and the smile of a lass!

They've told me the sky may be falling
and shown me a piece of it too.
Disaster must follow disaster,
there's not a darn thing we can do!
But I've not been hit by one yet
and know all these things too will pass,
so, here's to occasional fortune,
good luck and the smile of a lass!

My attitude may seem unhealthy,
yet it helps to keep me alive;
how could a poor optimist ever
have hope dashed each day and still thrive?
Oh, life does go on, after all;
I'll smile for you, I'm not an ass,
and toast to occasional fortune,
good luck and the smile of a lass!

MY GIRL

She was my girl
for a while
and I loved her more
than any before
or since. But that's
okay, you know?
It's good that there was
someone and a time
when I could call her
my girl.

She was my girl
and I was young
for the last time,
that golden summer, not long
ago, one golden
summer when love
fled before time's winds.
Still, I remember—
I could call her
my girl.

OUR SONG

I'm restless this evening, restless to hit
that road. It calls my name, a lover
I tried to forget. I can't
forget, kid. You know by now

I'm not the guy who will hold you
by the fire, share a joint
and a song, desiring nothing
more than the night. It's not enough;

only she can take me where
my dreams live. Sing for me
once more as the fire fades.
Sing our song and I shall go.

THERE

I get there
when I get there
and when I get there
it's no better there
than here

THE LAST ICE CREAM

The last ice cream of summer
melted along the curbs of suburban
streets, as bicycles lay
waiting on the neighbors' lawn,

waiting to take us on one
more adventure. How far could
we pedal? Across the tracks
(where we weren't supposed to go)

or only up the street to the park—
it really was up the street;
we coasted most of the way back
beneath the supple shade of half-grown

maples. I would not listen
for that jingle and that song
next summer; I would not know
where to look. The last

ice cream of summer was truly
the last ice cream of summer,
summer that came only once
and never returned.

ARRIVING

Crumbling asphalt gave way
to lime-rock further from town
and every fence-post stood
sentinel. I could not
tell you what sort of cattle
watched disinterestedly;
Santa Gertrudis I can recognize,
and Brahma, but not those
square, dun grazers.
The house is up ahead,
you told me. I could see
the sun on the tin roof,
or was that a barn?
Surely there was a barn.
Tired giants sprawled
into the yard, resting
fern-clad arms before
the porches. You waited there,
as sere fields all around
awaited rain. And I? I am
always arriving, always
leaving, already gone.
I see you waving, on the porch.
There will be lemonade.

COFFEE

Breakfast. Again, you did not
make enough coffee for both
of us. Too used to being
alone, I suppose, to pouring

out a cup or two for yourself
as you do your morning doings.
Each of those little acts
adds up to a performance

of life-goes-on, of work
now and we'll see each other
later on, maybe tomorrow night?
Whatever. It's all the same

to me, the guy going nowhere.
Right now, that road leads
through you and probably
past you to another

empty space, another roadside
stop where I will try to rest
and maybe find some change
for the coffee machine.

DISTANCE

There were days I knew I loved you
and long nights I feared I didn't.
There were burdens I chose to carry,
jealous lovers who spared no room

in my heart. Distance is distance;
it can not, could not, be made less
by all the aches of our longing.
What is love without the promise

of forever? Who am I
to demand such permanence?
There were days I should have loved you
and not cared for tomorrow.

SWIMMING

As the shark that must keep swimming
(yes, I know that is a fable),
so I could not breathe were I
motionless, no longer able

to move forward. Soon enough comes
rest and then we move no more,
strive no longer. In its time,
in its time, and not before,

shall I so rest. A mindless hunger
drives the shark: to eat, to mate,
to continue. That is all.
My seas are not so clear. My fate

is in these currents, bearing me
across the days I may not number.
No scent of blood has kept me swimming,
drawn me from the shores of slumber

I so fear; no, naught but my own
need to span the night, complete
this journey, swim till there is no
more need. Swim on till each defeat

and victory has faded, slipped
beyond the grasp of all the fates,
into dark, elusive depths,
and only an end awaits.

REST STOP

Why did you love if you did not intend
to love forever? Couldn't I be more
than just another stop along the road,

one more attraction to experience?

You've kept on traveling, I fear, too long
and missed the one place where you might have found
what rest this world has to offer you.

MARIPOSA

Brown girl with brown baby
and San Juan street ways
that would never be mine,

how came this *mariposa*
to my garden? I had
no nets to hold you.

Your smile was the sun;
your eyes told the secrets
of Caribbean depths.

RUBE

Rube Allyn wrote his stories
of the Water Wagon,
his home-made Best Bet houseboat,
when I was two years old

but the book was still
there on the shelf when I
reached reading age and dreaming
age, complete with schematics

and the smell of adventure
pressed between the pages.
There were lists of lumber
and fittings and maps to places

with names like Withlacoochee,
Okeechobee, even
Helen Blazes. I've been
to all of them since

and the names still whisper
their romance, remind
me of how I longed
for sky and open water.

My dad bought every one
of Rube's books, the reptile
and fish encyclopedias,
the yarns and histories

that were the Florida
of then and before then.
Paradise has faded;
faded like those pages.

CONCENTRATE

The smell of burnt oranges fills heaven,
rising with the caracara
from the prairie swamp. It is
a long, flat two-lane way from the coast

to Lake Okeechobee, broken only
by Immokalee, sleeping still
when I drove through. But the plants
run all night, up by the lake,

turning the golden fruit to juice,
concentrating Florida
for consumption. Pillar of smoke,
pillar of fire, lead me on,

though I know not why I was chosen,
no more than the high-humped Brahma cattle
that watch me pass, the red-wing singing
in the ditch. As time passes, unobserved,

all that is me is concentrated
here, on a road that leads
to dawn. Why question what may lie
beyond this smell of oranges?

SCALLOPING

The sea-grass seems almost black
at this depth. A cold hand gently
presses. I look up at blue distortions.

To my business. They are easy
to see if one knows how. There,
the sand settles, barely perceptible,

marking a passage. My gloved fingers
slip another scallop into the net
bag trailing at my waist.

Up for breath, all the way up,
not just through the snorkel.
Where is the boat? Momentary

disorientation. Used to that.
I prefer the shallows, I think,
wading the flats that seem

to extend forever into the warm
Gulf waters, green-straw, the gulls
wheeling and wheeling.

Down again, to depths of filtered
summer sun, to dark grass beds barely
acknowledging the sluggish current.

Nothing marks my passage, here,
a parting of water, a parting
of life, all flowing in behind.

CAYO HUESO
a song

Cayo Hueso, the Spaniards named it,
The isle as dry as a bone;
Sometimes dozing peacefully,
Sometimes by hurricanes blown.
They left it as they found it then,
'Neath a lonely sky,
Where the tropic sun still burns
And the frigate birds fly.

But others came to claim Key West,
Came down from the States,
And Yankee seamen built their port
Upon the Florida Straits.
It's where the Atlantic meets the Gulf,
And southward, Cuba lies;
The world lay beyond the horizon,
Just beyond their eyes.

We're sailing down to old Key West,
Down the mangrove coast;
Sailing down to harbor there
'Long side a smuggler's ghost.
I'll show you round my old Key West,
She is a gracious host;
So pour the rum and sailors all,
Let us raise a toast
To Cayo Hueso, (to Cayo Hueso!)
To old Key West.

The pendent on an island necklace,
Gem of the Florida keys:
Gold and jade and amethyst,
Set in the turquoise seas.
Audubon had tarried there
And Papa Hemingway;
When I get back to old Key West
I'll be there to stay.

THE CONSTANT STAR

On this voyage from nowhere
to nowhere, I'll fix the stars,
draw my charted sky
with you the constant north.

No wind blows more darkly
than yesterday's, when phantom
sails slipped the horizon.
In folly, have I pursued

such prizes, sought the siren
on her shore, dallied
over long in nameless
ports beyond the night.

Set the course, my star,
and I shall know your light;
it will shine a path
across the seas of my life.

POPEYE

My girlfriends keep dumping me
for boring guys. It seems the very
things that first attract them, first
interest them, must drive them

away, in time. But, like Popeye,
I yam what I yam. Even
sung asleep by these siren ports,
even if I pretend otherwise,

I'll never be otherwise;
I'll always be leaving me sweetie
for the sea. Olive, you're better
off with Bluto. I'm outa spinach.

SHIPS

I build ships in the desert
waiting for the rain
that is in your hands.
Open them.

MADE IN CHINA

It was a mysterious land,
an ancient land of silk
and oddly shaped mountains.
It evoked the exotic

when I was a child,
unknown, untouchable,
save through curios
and plates kept on high shelves.

The Great Wall has given
way to the great Walmart,
marking our new borders,
and 'Made in China' has lost

its wonder. No caravans
traverse the Silk Road, today.
No barques bear chests of fragrant
dragon tea to our docks.

I have held the teak
and jade of another age.
I remember when
there was a land of mystery.

EMBRACE

It is not far, this place we're bound,
just over the hill or maybe the next.
Across these fields, through these woods,
awaits night's welcoming embrace.

And it is heavy, that pack you filled
with all your broken bits of life.
Let loose the straps and run into
night's ever welcoming embrace.

PATH

We need follow a path
if we are to find
the place our own path begins.

Beyond the woods the way
is open. We will see
stars set high to guide us

and a sun that rises
above the fields we seek.

HOME PORT

Some men may seek the distant shore,
They need new worlds to explore;
But I would know the land that lies
Still unexplored behind your eyes.

I'll set my course by your bright star,
I'll ever seek you from afar,
Till I find rest upon your shore
And sail away in search no more.

Then, having dared across my sea,
A world's wonders call to me:
All your delights I might discover,
The secrets whispered to a lover.

To cup the curve of your fair breast,
Upon its pillow take my rest,
To kiss the hollow of your hand—
This would be my desired land.

WITH YOU

With you, I have sought
the elusive illusions
of life and love and learning,
of laughter and of thought.

With you, I have wondered
at a glory of stars
and an ache of hearts
from heaven's promise sundered.

Oh, we have been clever
yet unable to see
happiness lasts a moment,
forgetting is forever.

With you, I have fashioned
dreams from failing hope,
made our rumpled bed,
fevered and impassioned.

And with you, I've grown cold
standing in the moment,
waiting for tomorrow's
story to be told.

Oh, we have been so clever
yet unable to see
happiness lasts a moment,
forgetting is forever.

COUNT

I have loved too little and too much,
knowing not were you my sun or moon;
craved to feel the enigmatic touch
of nightfall even at the golden noon.
Your mirror eyes tell me not whether such
be seen for visionary or buffoon;
but I, as any dream-filled fool, must clutch
at my reflection, lest it fade too soon.

My fated path is plotted on this chart,
constant to your moon's erratic flight;
hold no silent promise in your heart,
make no wish upon the eve's first light.
Who knows the tides on which our ships depart?
Who hopes to count the stars before the night?

SIGNALS

Thunder and omens
you ask of me,
signs and wonders.
I am only I.
My signals come
on the feet of mice,
scurrying in the night,
on the fitful winds
of a clouded morn.
Listen.

ACROSS MY HORIZON

You sailed across my horizon,
found harbor in my heart.
A dismal place, I know,
a shabby little port
that few would bother visit
and those who do, depart
on tomorrow's tides.
Your days here will be short,

I know you can not stay.

I would dwell here no longer,
where memory laps my shore;
Could you give me passage
when you sail once more

across my horizon, away?

ONWARD

I.

You are another regret
in a life of regrets,
another wound that healed

but left its mark,
its scar to remind me
where I once hurt.

II.

Life may be defined
by those we love,
those we used to love,

those we will love.
All the rest is empty,
the meaningless dream.

III.

I have never plucked the rose,
not for fear of thorn
but that I would love too much;

when her sweetness faded
from the fickle air,
would I still be?

IV.

Time is our sole road
through the eternal desert;
nothing lives nor dies

beyond its pavements;
nothing loves nor hurts
unless it travel onward.

FORGOTTEN ISLE

a song

Dawn creeps up from the red-stained East,
Gulls mount to the skies;
My world's aflame on a day with no name,
As I watch the hot sun rise.

A forgotten man, a forgotten isle,
Lost in a steamy sea;
Here the days flow as the trade winds blow,
Away, away from me.

My life now seems but a verse
Of half-remembered song:
Without a rhyme and out of time,
But running on and on.

Though the world yet goes around
And days pass into years,
Without a care and bound nowhere,
Some tide has set me here.

GREEN MYSTERY

The sea, in her green mystery—
all my life, I've feared to love her.
At least three times she has come close

to killing me. Mother Ocean,
femme fatale, I have drunk deep
of her, breathed deep the salt of her air.

Where is your ship bound? I would
take passage to some other water,
some other woman, who would love

as I love. Each sailor needs
his port, his home, when voyaging
is done. I'll stop my ears then to

her siren singing and sail no more.
The sea, in her green mystery—
Is she the only love I'll know?

THE SAILOR'S LOVE

I. The Girl of the Islands

Tonight,
this golden, tropic night,
I sing you,
and each star that shines

reflects in the languid lagoon
where we swam
clothed only in our love.
Will you return

to me someday,
when your voyages of discovery
are done?

II. The Sailor on the Sea

Tonight,
this amethyst evening,
one star stands
above the empty sea.

My heart longs
to set a course by it,
yet the wind that fills my sails
carries me away,

away from you,
even as it whispers
your name.

WE SAIL, TONIGHT
a song

The wind blows nor' nor' east, tonight,
Not fit for man nor beast, tonight.
The thin clouds fly 'cross a darkened sky,
The moon waned to its least, tonight.

Our ship is outward bound, tonight,
To sea without a sound, tonight.
The tide runs high, the hawsers sigh
And dark lies close around, tonight.

A sure wind fills the sail, tonight,
A cold wind tells a tale, tonight.
It whispers why men strive and die;
Each song we raise must fail, tonight.

To distant ports, away, tonight,
Horizons far and gray, tonight.
The sea birds cry, the dawn we spy,
As we sail into day, from night.

DAWN
a song

Dawn was a tale the sea-birds told,
Against the eastern sky;
Dawn was a song of rose and gold
That could not tell me why

The night yet lingered in my heart
While day gloried above.
Each night, in dream, I once more part
From my too distant love.

On wind-swept shores, I hold her near,
Before I leave her side;
From wind-swept shores of home I steer
To seek a siren tide.

And one pale star, the Morning Star,
Then asked all I desired.
Oh, Morning Star, I would be far
Away, for I have tired

Of wandering the endless seas
With none to share my berth,
Of wandering where I may please
But finding naught of worth.'

In silence, my star faded then
Against the eastern sky;
In silence, I joined all those men
Who ask no more than 'why?'

WALK LIKE A SAILOR
a song

Walk like a sailor, roll with the waves,
pace your decks with pride;
the seas are growing in the gale,
we must go with the tide.

Pray for a strong and steady wind,
a star to be our guide;
we voyage far and the empty seas
that we shall sail are wide.

Walk like a sailor, walk like a sailor,
and never forget who you are;
cross your oceans without fear,
a true son of Jack Tar.

Walk like a sailor, walk like a sailor,
who's traveled the world 'round;
though you stop at a thousand ports,
you know where you are bound.

And when you stroll your native shore,
your true love at your side,
walk like a sailor, yes, like a sailor,
a swagger in your stride.

A MERRY MARINER
a song

I am a merry mariner, I am a jolly tar;
And I have seen all seven seas, I've sailed my ship afar.
Just let me have a seasoned crew, a craft that's sleek and yar;
I'll voyage from the Southern Cross up to the bright North Star.
Across the southern sea I'll chart a course to Zanzibar,
Then eastward to the Indies coast and ports in Malabar,
Or 'round the Cape, perhaps, I'll steer my long way to Dakar;
Though all the storms of Africa might rage, they'd be no bar.

Oft have I sought the unknown East to trade with the Chinese;
Returning then, my cargo chests of fragrant dragon teas,
Or laden with a hold of precious carven ivories,
The porcelains and silks of oriental treasuries.
Oh, I have lived a life as free as any ocean breeze;
The riches that I value most now are my memories.
And I have sailed and I have harbored when and where I please,
For no one is my master save the Lord of all the seas.

I've kept my solitary watch on nights so clear, I swear,
The stars rose up the sky like angels climbing heaven's stair,
Till morning overflowed the day, a dawning hot and fair;
The sun filled up the tropic sea and boiled into the air.
I'd sing a shanty as I worked beneath its ruthless glare,
And though the life be hard I've not found better anywhere.
A merry mariner am I, a tar who yet must fare
Across the sea's horizon mists to learn what might lie there.

I RESTED

For a time, I rested
on unknown coasts;
there a port lies hidden
between the arms of the mountains,
reaching like a lover
toward the uncaring sea.

Hear the songs calling,
plaintive in the streets
of night, in the dark cantinas
where sailors forget their ships.
It is I they call.
It is I who yearns.

The journey from me to you
began where another ended,
where tides rise and fall
unnoted. It is the way
of quests and dreams to fade so,
one into another.

Hear the sea calling;
I am timbers and sails,
straining to know the wind.
It tells of other ports;
it speaks of other coasts.
For a time, I rested.

PILLAR OF SALT

Guidepost to a land
I can not revisit,
You stand on my borders,
singing to the past.

Time's erosion slowly
carries you away,
taking each regret
on its desert winds,

every memory,
to the sullen sea.
I shall not look back;
only wastes remain.

FLOTSAM

I am cast up on your shores,
flotsam, wave-worn memories
of the man I was, the sailor
of dark seas and broken days.

Gather me. Among the polished
pearled shells, I wait, a dreaming
on the margins of tomorrow.
Once we found such remnants, there,

tokens of the unseen storm.
Call to your horizons, misted
with the songs of pasts forgotten;
all that we have yearned for lies

sleeping in the distant blue
reaches, lies yet undiscovered.
Might you sail to such a venture,
taking ship along the curve

of a restless golden morn?
Might you rise across your days?
I remain, on shores a world
distant, discard, sea-gift, flotsam

drifted from unvoyaged depths.
Find me there, someday, among
treasures of the tide; then hold me
to your ear to hear my song.

ANCHOR

She was my anchor when I thought
I needed one, when I sought
stability in another
I could not find within myself.
And when the gale arose she let
go the chain, let me drift
away to ride my storm alone.
Now tempests I have weathered and found
I need no anchor, only the wind,
only the sky and the sea,
only this ship, only life.

VOYAGER

I will not reach for that I can not hold,
nor will I trade tomorrow for a moment
once glimpsed in ocean mirrors. Far, you lie,
across the seas of blue imagination,

too distant for our cargoed truth to sail.
Drink up, my mates, to those who chanced the storm,
for every voyager makes port or drowns
and life's the better part of any profit.

TOMORROW'S SEA

Dreamer, sail with me, across tomorrow's sea;
we both know this wind that blows for you and me.
Choose one distant light and tell it who we are;
take the helm, then, dreamer, steer us by that star.

Lonely have I voyaged on this sea before,
dreaming toward that harbor on its distant shore.
Captain of night's barque, in mists I've sought and sailed;
always it lay hidden, always have I failed.

Dreamer, can you see the hills above a cove,
sea-birds rising dawn-ward, rest for those who rove?
No more must we, yearning, sail a nameless sea
of regrets and losses; dreamer, seek with me.

THE WAVE, SPENT

The wave, spent, whispers memories
of its journey, of ice-edged winds
that gave it birth in distant, arctic
seas, the winds that nourished, strengthened,

sent it forth to test its power
upon these shores. It speaks of schools
of slender silver-sided fish,
darting, dazzling, and great whales

in cold green depths below. The gulls
have played along its crest, harsh cries
rising, fading, filled with tales
forever lost to the horizon.

Sky and waters, tumult, tempest;
ships that labored against a vast
and timeless ocean—all these has
it seen, and then warm tropic currents,

stars that blazed in constellations
unsuspected on northern coasts.
To strive here, crash against the painted
coral reefs is destiny,

to gather strength, rush from the deep,
and broken, reach an end, at last.
The sand has heard it all before;
it lets the foam slip back, and away.

WIND

Wind was a god, creating, destroying, moving
upon the water. Each moonlit ripple held
its universes, impermanent reflections

appearing, dissipating, into night.
What infinite worlds shine and die before us,
what bits and pieces of reality?

All fades; dark seas of entropy lie calm
once more and what could be has been. Remember
the wind. Remember what you can, and sleep.

I WAS

I was a sailor, voyaging
upon the shoreless sea;
I was a soldier, conquering
each upstart enemy.
And ever did I question why
all of these things must be;
no answer served to satisfy
the hungers roused in me.

I was a lover, seeking one
who might fulfill my days;
I was a fugitive, undone
by my own lawless ways.
And I have walked, in search of dreams,
such paths to which life strays
when man, with desperate want, it seems,
believes not yet he prays.

I was all this, I was all men,
the many with one name,
while all that is and that has been
went even as it came.
In generations have I sailed,
I've marched to follow fame,
and I have won and I have failed
and now it's all the same.

SAIL

Traveler, I, seeking the words
that make tomorrow.

Explorer, voyager,
my Fountain of Truth

lies beyond this shrouded
horizon, just beyond

the mists, where the sea
plummets to eternity.

Sail with me; the edge
of the world beckons

to a restless soul.

Thank you for voyaging with me. I hope you have enjoyed this collection of my poems. ~ *Stephen Brooke*

Stephen Brooke is a poet, novelist, artist, and sometime surfer, residing in the Florida Panhandle. http://stephenbrooke.com

Other poetry titles by Stephen Brooke,
all available from the Arachis Press:
　Pieces of the Moon
　Dreamwinds
　Retellings
　The Tower
　Fields of Summer
　Awful Alvin and Other Peculiar Poems (Juvenile)

Eggshell Boats is an imprint of the Arachis Press
http://eggshellboats.com
http://arachispress.com

www.ingramcontent.com/pod-product-compliance
Lightning Source LLC
Chambersburg PA
CBHW051714040426
42446CB00008B/878